THE ABLE-BODIED SEAMAN

Alan Bowne

BROADWAY PLAY PUBLISHING INC
New York
www.broadwayplaypublishing.com
info@broadwayplaypublishing.com

THE ABLE-BODIED SEAMAN

Cover photo of Alan Bowne, Stuyvesant Square, N Y C, in 1976

First edition: October 2017
I S B N: 978-0-88145-710-0

Book design: Marie Donovan
Page make-up: Adobe InDesign
Typeface: Palatino

CHARACTERS & SETTING

ROY BONINO, *a merchant seaman, in his 40s*
FAY, *his daughter, 16*
RITA, *his friend, about 40*
MANFRED, *his friend, in his 40s*
BOGART, *boyfriend to* FAY, *19*
PHILIP GAMBLE, *a lawyer, in his late 20s*

ROY BONINO'*s apartment in Queens, New York. A single
set. A large central space, with table, chairs, T V, day bed,
kitchenette and counter, divided from a small bedroom area.
The central room is grimy, parched, ill-painted, with little
embellishment beyond a travel poster of Sicily on the wall.
Entrance door from landing at back of stage, a window
looking onto the fire escape at left. The bedroom area is
reached through a doorframe with beaded curtain and it is
lighter and frillier, with bed and vanity, everything strewn
with feminine underclothes. A Snoopy pillow. A door leads
from bedroom to offstage bathroom.*

Time: One hot muggy day in the summer.

ACT ONE: *Morning*
ACT TWO: *That afternoon*
ACT THREE: *That night*

NOTE

The unorthodox spelling and punctuation are intentional, indicating the pronunciation, and the breathing, specific to the New York City idiom employed.

ACT ONE

(*Morning. In the central room, the daybed is mussed and a duffel bag is gutted in one corner. A scotch bottle and glass on table.*)

(ROY BONINO, *in undershirt and khakis, is rummaging in overstuffed closet.*)

(*In bedroom,* FAY, *not visible to* ROY, *enters from bathroom wrapped in a towel. She sits at vanity and fusses.*)

ROY: (*Over his shoulder*) Fay? So where's my blue suit?

FAY: (*Fussing at vanity*) I told you when you got in last night.

ROY: Got a lot on my mind here!

FAY: I told you, I put your whole thing in the closet.

ROY: (*Rummaging*) I come home and I got no bedroom no more?

FAY: Did I tell you? I'm sixteen, I need the bedroom, it's a privacy thing.

ROY: You didn't tell me fuckall last night, Fay. Your old man's first night home and he gets what, what's he get? He gets, can't go bowling with you, Dad, I gotta date how do I look good-bye eat me.

FAY: You was high as a kite and I don't bowl no more.

ROY: Such a big girl we got here, so where's my egg? You don't bowl no more so you throw out my egg? And my blue suit, it's at the cleaners?

FAY: Dad, it's in there.

(A knocking at entrance door; they ignore it)

ROY: get a peck onna nose and I'm livin in the front room now.

FAY: So get us a bigger apartment.

ROY: *(Pulls out suit)* Here it is. *(While hanging it up on closet door:)* Just get off my back this apartment, Fay. I told you, we're gettin a house.

(Another knocking)

FAY: Answer the door.

ROY: *(Ignoring knock, trying on suit)* Privacy? You will have privacy up the ass.

FAY: Jesus. *(She rises from vanity and exits back into bathroom, slamming door)*

ROY: And a telephone answer machine! *(In suit jacket, rummages again in closet, on all fours)* So my egg is where? Fay? Twenny-four hours a day you're inna bathroom, Fay.

(Another, sharper knocking)

ROY: Just like your mother was!

(FAY sticks her head out of bathroom.)

FAY: *(Yelling it)* So Dad! Will you get the fuckin door? *(She disappears into bathroom again.)*

(ROY groans, stops rummaging, moves to entrance door.)

ROY: God-damned lousy foulmouth young broad with her mouth *(Opens door on RITA)* Rita.

RITA: Roy!

ROY: So?

RITA: *(Holding out edible in cellophane)* I brung you a knish.

ROY: For what?

RITA: For breakfast.

ROY: *(Staring at it)* A knish.

RITA: You wanted a gyro?

(ROY, exasperated, turns back to closet and resumes rummaging, as RITA enters and crosses, bustling, to kitchenette.)

RITA: I didn't know you was back, Roy, til Fay stuck a note under my door. You coulda called, Roy.

ROY: Lot on my mind.

RITA: It's so hot today, turn on a fan. *(Opens fridge, looks inside)* Two bananas? And a chocolate milk? Fay. Is not. Domestic.

(Meanwhile FAY has emerged from bathroom into bedroom in her slip. She now enters central room through beaded curtain, still in her slip.)

FAY: Rita. This is a scorcher what do you think?

RITA: Fay, you look awful I gotta say it.

ROY: *(Rummaging deeper into closet)* You would too, you was out dancin all night.

FAY: *(Picking up bottle from table)* Dad, you gonna juice out today, or what?

ROY: *(Coming out of closet)* Put that down, that's for a very important business meeting I'm havin here today.

FAY: With who? You, you, and your feet?

ROY: *(Disappearing back into closet)* Don't worry *about* it!

FAY: *(Slamming down bottle, crossing to kitchenette)* What? Me? Worry? *(Pointing at cellophane; to RITA)* What's this?

RITA: A knish, you wanna knish?

FAY: *(Shaking her head, disgusted)* Jesus.

RITA: You should eat breakfast, Fay.

FAY: *(Making instant coffee)* I don't want breakfast.

RITA: You wanna banana?

(FAY shakes her head.)

RITA: Chocolate milk?

(FAY shakes her head.)

RITA: I could go upstairs. I got Grape Nuts.

(FAY shakes her head.)

RITA: A Pop Tart you wanna Pop Tart?

ROY: *(Jerking out of closet, exasperated) Pop it out your ass!*

FAY: Don't talk ugly at Rita!

ROY: Where's my egg??

FAY: I don't know!

ROY: Why don t you know?

FAY: *(Ignoring her father; to RITA, embracing her)* Rita, how long you been comin down here and askin me. Do I want breakfast?

RITA: A coupla years. Ever since your mother. *(Glances pointedly at ROY)* Left. And didn't. Come back.

(ROY grumbles and disappears again into closet, rummaging.)

FAY: Right. You been like a mother to me. I love your guts I could eat you alive. But Rita?

RITA: Fay?

FAY: *(Ending embrace)* I will never. Eat. Breakfast.

ROY: *(From inside closet)* When'd you get in last night?

FAY: *(Sipping coffee)* Who?

ROY: When was that, Fay?

FAY: You was out passed fuckin stewed.

ROY: You out there gettin in trouble?

FAY: *(Shaking head)* Jesus. *(To* RITA*)* Already I'm sweating I just took a shower.

ROY: You out there gettin pregnant?

FAY: Don't be gross. I'm onna pill what year were you born?

ROY: Onna what'?

FAY: Pill.

ROY: Pill?

RITA: *(Hissing into closet)* The birth control!

*(*ROY *bursts out of closet.)*

ROY: *That makes it better????!*

FAY: Stop yellin at her, Dad.

ROY: So what's this pill shit?

RITA: *(Thrusting knish at* ROY, *who pushes it away)* Eat something, Roy. *(Then offers it to* FAY*)* Fay, you gotta eat.

FAY: *(Gulping coffee)* Gotta get to class.

ROY: *Class?*

FAY: Modelling class.

ROY: What kinna *model*?!

FAY: It's a modelling class in Flushing gotta get dressed. Somebody's comin by to pick me up. Rita thinks you should meet him.

RITA: You should, Roy.

ROY: What's his name?

FAY: He's a boy I know and maybe you *should* meet him. Very. Briefly.

ROY: He's Italian at least?

FAY: *(Crossing to bedroom)* I don't know from Italians, maybe he's Jewish.

ROY: Jewish is O K. He better not be a *tootsoon'*. *(Italo-American slang for "nigger")*

RITA: Roy! Go to confession.

FAY: Jesus.

(Exit FAY into bedroom; begins dressing, in and out of bathroom, etc., during following)

ROY: *(Sitting at table, reaching for bottle; to RITA)* A hot number, I get home and I got a hot number for a daughter.

RITA: She a lovely girl everyone says so. Where was you this trip?

ROY: *(Pouring himself a short one)* Yemen. So who is this guy?

RITA: Yemen? Is that like near Iran?

ROY: *(Knocking back drink, slamming glass to table)* Fuckin Iran! *(Beat)* So who's the boyfriend, Rita?

RITA: *(At counter, performing actions as she describes them)* Here, I'll pour you a glass of chocolate milk and this knish. On a napkin. Spread over a plate. Pretty. I'll split it put in some ketchup.

ROY: You gonna answer me, Rita?

(RITA moves downstage, sets plate and glass before ROY.)

RITA: Eat your knish it'll get cold.

ROY: Rita would you get that grease outa my face. And answer me?

RITA: Drink some chocolate.

ROY: *(Ominous)* Rita.

(RITA removes plate and glass.)

RITA: My god, you're this A B, Roy, it's beautiful.

ROY: A B so what? That stand for "Able-Bodied Slavehead."

RITA: *Seaman,* Roy. It's a wonderful thing to have a title like that.

ROY: Yeah, sure, someday I could be a wiper. If I'm lucky.

RITA: *(At counter again)* Good trip?

ROY: Biggest trip of my life.

RITA: Yeah?

ROY: Yeah. *(Looking into glass)* A man died out there.

(Pause)

RITA: *(Carefully setting down plate and glass)* That's awful. Who?

ROY: A young P R you don't know him. Fell from the top deck right down to the hold. Coulda been me.

RITA: Don't talk like this it's terrible.

ROY: Coulda been me would O'Farrell Lines give a dick? I could check out like that P R and O'Farrell would say. Another stupid seaman gets drunk and buys it he was a asswipe here's ten dollars don't bother us.

RITA: Don't dwell on it, Roy. Think good thoughts.

ROY: I'll think what I wanna think. And what I'm thinkin is money. For a house. In like Rockaway. Or Long Island. A nice house, like Fay always wanted.

RITA: Don't lose your dreams, Roy. And money? You're making good money Jesus Roy. Six months at home six months at sea it's wonderful.

ROY: Eat me.

RITA: Roy.

ROY: Eat me what else I could plug you up?

RITA: Roy.

ROY: (*Reaching again for bottle*) Lemme alone!

RITA: Roy, scotch anna empty stomach— (*Beat*) That's like— (*Beat*) Battery acid on Kleenex.

(ROY *splashes a little scotch into glass, caps bottle, pushes it away, and stares glumly at* RITA.)

RITA: We missed you, Roy.

(ROY *stares.*)

RITA: You know there's a block party?

(*Same*)

RITA: Rock bands and priests and everything. Its not San Gennaro but what do you want it's Corona Queens. Music. Booths. Zeppole.

ROY: (*Incredulous, looking away, downing drink*) Block party. The woman. Is yakkin block party.

(*There is the sound of a buzzer.*)

RITA: (*Crossing to box near entrance door*) I'll get it Roy don't get up.

ROY: Rita?

RITA: Bonino?

ROY: Tell me about this boy. Of Fay's.

RITA: (*Into box*) Who is it? (*Ear to box; pushes button. To* ROY) It's Manfred. I called him said you was back.

ROY: Tell me his name, Rita. Tell me his face.

RITA: (*Moving downstage to stand by T V*) Roy watch some television.

ROY: My daughter. Is a hot number all of a sudden.

RITA: A B C got the *Million Dollar Man* on reruns. Or a soap. You should soap, Roy. Dumb? All right. I'm not sayin a soap is for I Q. It's a personal thing, Roy. For the child in all of us.

ROY: *(Staring at her)* You're lunched. A walking lunchbucket.

(There is a knocking at entrance door.)

RITA: *(Moving upstage to entrance door)* I'll get it so don't worry.

(RITA admits MANFRED.)

MANFRED: Rita. Roy!

ROY: *(Rising)* Manfred hey!

(MANFRED and ROY meet and embrace, pounding each other on back.)

ROY: This here. Is just the guy I wanna see.

(Releasing MANFRED, ROY crosses to duffel, rummages for papers.)

ROY: Wanna check some figures with you, Manfred.

FAY: *(At beaded curtain)* Hey, Manfred.

MANFRED: Fay! Look at this. Your dad's back.

FAY: I noticed. You ain't been around in awhile.

MANFRED: Been up to see Rita. But she said you was kinna— *(Suggestive) Busy* down here, so—

ROY: *(Jerking round, papers in hand)* Kinna *what?*

RITA: *(Hissing it, a warning)* Manfred!

(FAY exits quickly into bedroom.)

(ROY stares ominously at MANFRED.)

MANFRED: *(Nervously, to RITA)* Hot it's hot. Humidity at eighty-nine percent. Turn on the A/C. *(Moving to table; to ROY)* When'd you get back? Heard you was back it's all over Queens out to the 59th Street welcome home.

(ROY *crosses to table, casts papers onto it, and stares at his friends, darkly*)

RITA: *(To* MANFRED, *nervously)* I think the A/C's broke.

MANFRED: So turn on a fan.

RITA: I asked him to turn on a fan.

MANFRED: And he didn't turn one on?

RITA: I asked him.

MANFRED: You mentioned the fan.

RITA: I made a special point.

MANFRED: So why didn't he?

RITA: I dunno.

(Beat, as MANFRED *and* RITA *look at* ROY*)*

ROY: *(Nodding rapidly)* O K. *(Beat; nodding rapidly)* O K. *(Beat; he sits, nodding rapidly; in one breath:)* O K. O K. O K.

MANFRED: *(Also sitting at table)* So uh. Early. *(Taps bottle)* For this.

*(*ROY *leans forward to stare at* MANFRED, *ominous.)*

MANFRED Hey! At the block party tonight? This kumquat.

RITA: *(Fussing at counter)* You and your kumquats. You want somethin to eat?

MANFRED: *(Ignoring* RITA; *to* ROY, *warming to subject, leering)* Very juicy. And I want you should meet her.

(No response from ROY*)*

MANFRED: Sure. I want she should know that you and me? Are just, these two guys. Completely neighborhood. And totally Queens. *(Beat; embarrassed)* You know, the borough.

(Still no response from ROY*)*

MANFRED: It's very impressive, Roy, you bein this seaman and so on and so forth. Me, I own a store it ain't the same thing.

(ROY *shakes his head in disbelief.*)

MANFRED: So Roy.

ROY: *(Slow burning)* Yeah?

MANFRED: Good trip?

ROY: No.

MANFRED: Me too.

RITA: *(To* MANFRED*)* What do you mean, you too?

MANFRED: Me. *(Beat)* Too.

RITA: You too what? He says no and you says you too.

MANFRED: Yeah, that right.

ROY: *(Head in hands)* Jesus.

(To ROY*)*

MANFRED: At the store yesterday? That was uh. Friday. A big day. We sold what? A parakeet.

RITA: New Yorkers love animals how could you not make a profit?

MANFRED: A parafreet. Maybe a hampster.

RITA: New Yorkers love animals they will murder you inna street you mistreat a dog.

MANFRED: A box of birdfeed.

RITA: I can't understand this it's impossible.

ROY: *(Exploding) Port Au'tority!*

(Beat; MANFRED *and* RITA *stare at* ROY*)*

MANFRED: Roy?

ROY: *I'm at the Port Au'tority!* These buses comin in. People from asshole middle of shit. Talkin block party.

Talkin kumquat. (*Leans across table; into* MANFRED'*s face*) Talkin birdseed and my *daughter*? She's kinna *busy* down here!

MANFRED: Roy. I didn't mean nothin by that.

RITA: Roy, with Fay it's like. Puppy love.

ROY: It's what?

RITA: As innocent as the tush on a newborn baby at a baptism.

ROY: Yeah? Well, it *better* be, Rita!

MANFRED: Roy. This. (*Indicating bottle*) Is delapitating. (*Author intends this should be mispronounced.*)

(ROY *falls forward, exasperated, onto table, head in arms.*)

RITA: (*Moving downstage with plate*) He should eat.

MANFRED: Sure, puts hair on your chest. What's that?

RITA: (*Showing plate to* MANFRED) It's a knish.

MANFRED: He don't want it?

RITA: You want it?

MANFRED: You put mustard?

RITA: Ketchup.

MANFRED: Ketchup why you put ketchup onna knish?

RITA: Some people like ketchup.

MANFRED: That like. Mayonnaise onna frank.

RITA: He don't got any mustard! So I put ketchup!

(ROY *springs to his feet, smashing his glass to the floor.*)

ROY: *I come here!* I am onna tub fulla mongoloids for six fuckin months and I come here! My daughter turns hot in six lousy months and my neighbors are from Mars! I go to Tashkent and I come back to Queens, what is this shit? (*Beat*) Huh? What is. This shit? (*Silence. He sits, picking up papers.*) I got a business appointment today.

Gotta have a. Strategy. *(Waving papers)* I'm talkin.
Bucks here.

MANFRED: *(Nodding)* This is finance.

ROY: Yeah.

MANFRED: You got some heavy thinkin.

ROY: Very heavy. A man is comin here. A uh. Attorney.

MANFRED: A lawyer.

ROY: Yeah.

RITA: Roy what you want a lawyer?

ROY: Like he said. It's finance.

MANFRED: Sure. You gotta have a lawyer you move in those circles.

RITA: Roy where you get enough finance you need a lawyer?

MANFRED: I open my store I hadda have one. My brother hadda lawyer he closed out his house in Astoria. You don't wipe yourself without a lawyer.

RITA: I been wipin myself all my life I never need a lawyer.

(Quickly:)

MANFRED: You're a woman.

RITA: So?

MANFRED: You're a woman.

RITA: So?

MANFRED: You're a woman. *(No pause)* Hey. Roy. Get your percentage.

ROY: Manfred, will you lissen to me?? Your brother. He still talkin that car service?

MANFRED: Yeah, only its hard to find partners, Roy. It's a tight money marketplace today.

ROY: So he'd let me go in with him?

MANFRED: Sure, if you got the capital. But it's a big investment, Roy. We're talkin thirty, forty g's here.

ROY: That what I wanna know. *(Begins figuring on paper)* We're talkin a good fifty percent return on, say, like, thirty-five?

MANFRED: *(Impressed)* That's a nice round number.

ROY: So you can call him today and set it up?

MANFRED: Sure. Roy, this is great. You gonna get rich?

ROY: *(Figuring)* I'm gonna be. What you call. Comfortable.

RITA: Roy, they make you captain of the ship or somethin? A car service is a big businessy kinna thing, Roy. Strictly for overcoats.

MANFRED: *(To RITA)* What are you, anti-Italian defamation? A car service, Queens to Manhattan, what's it take? A storefront, a phone, and you got the numbers onna side. It's a once-in-a-lifetime.

RITA: Don't you gotta have a fleet for this? Limos and pay-offs and that?

MANFRED: Would you fuck yourself? My brother is a well-connected man! *(To ROY)* You couldn't do better with your money.

ROY: And then it's good-bye Corona hello Rockaway. With sprinklers onna lawn. *(Stops figuring, raises bottle)* Let's drink on it!

MANFRED: Hey, no thanks. But this is great, Roy. I'm happy here.

ROY: So drink with me! Rita, bring over some glasses.

MANFRED: No, can't do it, Roy. Gotta be in trim this kumquat.

ROY: *(Man of the world)* You're wastin your time all that.

MANFRED: All that what?

ROY: Bitches. You're wastin your time.

RITA: *(After a beat)* Roy.

ROY: Rita.

RITA: Was I just a bitch? To you?

(Beat, as ROY *rolls his eyes at* MANFRED*)*

RITA: So don't say that, Roy.

ROY: *(To* MANFRED*)* She's talkin fourteen years ago.

RITA: It wasn't no fourteen years, Roy.

ROY: A long time ago what's the point?

RITA: I wasn't no bitch, Roy. Not to you.

ROY: O K. O K. You wasn't no bitch.

(Beat)

MANFRED: You two wanna be alone?

*(*RITA *finds whisk and dustpan and moves downstage to clean up* ROY's *broken glass.)*

RITA: Thank you, Roy, cause I wasn't.

*(*RITA *begins sweeping up broken glass. To her:)*

ROY: Leave it. I'll get it later.

*(*RITA *continues.)*

ROY: I said—

RITA: This is broken glass, Roy. This is not plastic.

ROY: You are such a help.

RITA: I try to be. Somethin wrong with that?

ROY: Such a help you can right away clean this up. But clean up my daughter for six months? Forget it.

*(*RITA *moves upstage to kitchenette, dumps glass into wastebasket. As she does so:)*

RITA: What do you mean? I mean, what do you mean?

MANFRED: Now the pet business, Roy, it stinks.

(RITA *moves downstage with sponge.*)

ROY: *(To* RITA*)* I mean. I go away she's a little lady I come back she's a space heater. Is what I mean.

RITA: *(Bending over, sopping up liquid)* No. She's a good girl.

MANFRED: *(Appraising her)* Rita? You still got your body.

ROY: Is what I mean.

RITA: *(Straightening up)* Roy. I check on her every day. I see her off to school I drop by at night. She's a good. Girl. *(She returns to kitchenette.)*

MANFRED: It's the competition, Roy. People go to these. In Manhattan. These doggie boutiques? They want gerbils. Marmosets. They want dogs without assholes. That don't shit or smell.

ROY: Manfred?

MANFRED: Most guys run pet stores? Are faggots. But I am not a faggot and my dogs come with assholes.

ROY: I said: Manfred?

MANFRED: Mrs. Dorfman comes in wants to know. Why. You can't train her Shepard. To a catbox.

ROY: *You gonna give out with the gerbils all day???*

(The buzzer sounds.)

FAY: *(Out of bathroom)* It's for me!

(FAY emerges from bedroom, half-dressed. Leans on button)

ROY: *(To his daughter)* You gonna see him like that?

(FAY does not respond, exits into bedroom.)

MANFRED: O K, we talk finance. Now Roy. You buy into this deal with my brother? And you got a steady profit the rest of your life. If I had the money, I would jump at it.

ROY: But a guy should invest on toppa this, right? A house in Rockaway or some shit? Is upkeep.

MANFRED: Roy, you got your debentures, your futures, your I R As, your money market, your Keoghs—

ROY: *(Cutting him off)* Just call your brother, Manfred!

RITA: He's a nice boy, Bonino.

ROY: Who's a nice boy?

RITA: *(Gesturing at door)* This one. Want some coffee?

ROY: He's Italian?

RITA: No, he's white. Or maybe Irish.

ROY: He's in high school?

RITA: He's older.

ROY: An older man???

RITA: He's not even twenny.

ROY: And what?

RITA: And what what?

ROY: *And what does he do?*

RITA: *I didn't ask him!*

(A brisk knocking at entrance door.)

FAY: *(Calling from bedroom)* I'll get it!

(FAY, almost dressed, passes through beaded curtain, opens door.)

(Enter BOGART in a leather vest, no shirt, tight chinos, gold slave bracelet and construction boots. Chewing gum)

(BOGART embraces FAY playfully; she laughs and wriggles away.)

ROY: This. Is puppy love?

RITA: *(Waving to* BOGART*)* Hi, doll.

*(*BOGART *snaps his fingers in salutation at* RITA*.)*

FAY: *(To* BOGART*)* Come on in my dad's back.

ROY: *(To* MANFRED*)* He comes in here. And acts like this.

RITA: I'll make some coffee! *(She casts about for coffee stuff.)*

*(*FAY *brings* BOGART *downstage to table.)*

FAY: *(To* BOGART*)* This is my dad. *(Turns away; again to* BOGART*)* Come on in the bedroom I'm almost ready we'll go.

ROY: Hey.

*(*FAY *and* BOGART *pause.)*

ROY: His name? His address? He got a record?

*(*BOGART *spreads hands, feigning surprise.)*

ROY: They don't got a record on him? So why's he actin like this?

FAY: Dad.

ROY: You say to him, this is the old party who pays the bills. Funny, huh? So let's go inna bedroom act like he's a parapalegic. *(Author intends that this word be mispronounced.)*

RITA: Fay, introduce him around. For god's sake.

FAY: *(To herself)* Jesus. *(To* BOGART*)* This is my dad and this is Manfred he owns a pet store off the Major Deegan. Rita you met. *(Turning away again; again to* BOGART*)* So come on.

ROY: *(Exploding)* What's his name!

*(*FAY *and* BOGART *halt as* ROY *springs to his feet.)*

ROY: I don't wanna know from Manfred offa Major Deegan I *know* Manfred! I know Rita she lives upstairs! I know everybody this apartment cept I do *not*! *I repeat!* I do fuckin not know this leather vest with its titties hangin out! *(Jabbing finger at* FAY) So what. Is. His *name*?

BOGART: *(Quickly)* Bogart!

ROY: *(Staring at him)* Bo what?

BOGART: Bogart.

(ROY *looks at* RITA, *then at* MANFRED.)

ROY: His name. Is Bogart.

BOGART: I'm Bogart you're Mr Bonino. This here is Mr Manfred and over there is Rita. You gotta dog? You wanner introduce me?

MANFRED: I got just the dog would go with you.

ROY: *(To* BOGART) You think I'm funny.

BOGART: Hey. What did I do?

MANFRED: A pitbull.

BOGART: *(Extending hand)* So I'm happy to meet ya Mr Bonino. O K?

MANFRED: A pitbull is just the dog for a guy like this.

ROY: *(Staring at proffered hand; mean)* You prob'ly raped a queer with that hand.

(Pause)

BOGART: *(Slowly withdrawing hand)* I unnerstand. *(To* FAY) Hey. Do I unnerstand?

FAY: Dad. Easy up. You hear me?

BOGART: Sure, I unnerstand. You been on this banana boat since Christmas. It figures you'd be, you know. Irritatible. *(Author intends that this word should be mispronounced.)*

ROY: *(To* BOGART*)* Can you count on your fingers?

BOGART: *(Cold)* Sure. I'm a high-school graduate.

MANFRED: A pitbull is a beast.

ROY: *(Holding up finger; to* BOGART*)* So show me. One?

MANFRED: Clamps down on you you gotta get a lead pipe break his jaw.

FAY: Dad?

ROY: *(To* FAY*)* Shut up! *(To* BOGART*)* Come on, I said count. One?

BOGART: One.

ROY: And after that comes—?

BOGART: Two.

ROY: Two. Good. And when you get to five?

BOGART: This is not imagination.

ROY: You be on my stoop! Headin for the subway!

BOGART: *(Defiant; indicating* FAY*)* She can't get dressed that fast.

ROY: She ain't goin with you.

BOGART: Oh. I feature.

(FAY *turns angrily away, stomps upstage into bedroom.)*

BOGART: *(To* ROY*)* Anything else?

ROY: Yeah, there is. See, you been dick up this apartment for months, you think the lease is in your name. But I got news for you, blondie. Now on you gonna be somewhere else. Like at a pac-man game some place like where they sell dirty magazines? You can stand there. For the rest of your life. And play pac-man.

(BOGART *chews gum and looks at others, then at* ROY.)

BOGART: I don't play computer.

(Beat)

ROY: *(Gapes; then to* MANFRED) He don't play computer.

BOGART: I play pinball only.

RITA: *(smiling at* BOGART) And I bet you're very good at it.

*(*ROY *stares back and forth at* RITA *and* BOGART *during following)*

BOGART: *(To* RITA, *seductive)* Gotta use your body with pinball. *(Undulates, wrist extended)* Gotta move with it. Timing. it's all in the body. Computer is for pussies.

RITA: What do you mean?

BOGART: Like, you know, those kids with purple tennies and glasses. All this dumb shit printed on their shirts. *(Moving hand across chest)* Like, you know. "Denver."

RITA: Oh, right.

BOGART: Sure. Or you know. *(Moving hand across chest again)* "Hi. What's Your Name? My Name's Asshole."

RITA: You wanna knish?

ROY: *Rita!*

RITA: Bonino?

ROY: Rita you make the coffee *(In same breath, to* BOGART) you make me tired. I don't wanna see. Your pineapple hair. Or your vanilla boobies. On these premises. Anymore.

*(*ROY *and* BOGART *stare, as* RITA *rises hastily to make coffee at counter. Finally,* BOGART *turns defiantly away and moves upstage as* ROY *slowly descends into chair.)*

*(*FAY, *fully dressed, emerges from bedroom with danskin bag.)*

FAY: *(Pinching* BOGART's *behind)* Meet you at the corner.

BOGART: We gonna dance tonight, Fay.

FAY: We gonna sweat you better be ready.

BOGART: *You* be ready, Fay. Cause after the disco? I got a surprise for you.

(ROY leaps to his feet; to BOGART:)

ROY: I see you around here again?

(Lunges for BOGART; MANFRED restrains him.)

ROY: And I got a surpise for *you*, peaches!

MANFRED: Hold on, Roy.

FAY: *(Angrily, to ROY)* Will you fuckin cool out???

(MANFRED gets ROY, fuming, to sit.)

FAY: *(To defiant BOGART)* I said. At the corner.

(BOGART snaps his fingers in parting and exits.)

(FAY approaches table, looking at ROY.)

FAY: When you gonna let go?

ROY: Some kinna fruitbar or stumblebum some kinna J D juvie off a Queens Boulevard. Fucks you fucks his mother prob'ly a Protestant some shit.

MANFRED: Fucks his mother?

FAY: *(Exasperated, to MANFRED)* He don't fuck his mother *(In same breath to ROY)* would you fuck off with this? And he don't got a religion who's got a religion?

RITA: The religion of god.

MANFRED: The religion of god, what sorta puck-puck is that?

RITA: Everything is one banana.

ROY: *I'm waitin!* *(Beat)* In my own apartment I have to wait. My daughter with that *(Gesturing)* that dukie and you *(To RITA and MANFRED)* with your mouths. I have to wait for this in my own apartment.

FAY: Wait the christ for what?

ROY: Satisfaction!

MANFRED: Roy? I would hate to fuck up your satisfaction.

RITA: Roy's just. Irritatible.

ROY: Don't push it, Rita! *(Sits, pours a drink; to* FAY*)* So go. What l got planned for you so go. You rather would fuck some faggot J D? Go ahead and fuck him I hope you get hepatitus.

FAY: Plan?

ROY: For you. But go.

FAY: What you, you gonna take me to the Christmas Spectacular at Radio City?

ROY: *(Offhand, flat)* You fuckin dirt. Ungrate.

MANFRED: This is a sin.

RITA: He's a good dad one of the best, Fay.

MANFRED: Mondo superbo I always said it, Fay.

ROY: Kill yourselves.

MANFRED: Roy?

ROY: *Kill yourselves and go home!* (Beat; to FAY) So go. I'll spend it on somebody else.

FAY: Spend what?

ROY: I'm comin into money don't ask questions. You wanna hump a queer? That's alright with me.

FAY: I said: spend what?

ROY: *(Gesturing in air)* Five. Zero. Then one of those, you know. A squiggle. And zero. Zero. Zero.

RITA: Comma, it's a comma, Roy.

FAY: Fifty thousand dollars? How you gonna?

ROY: It's not for you to know, its for you to spend. Only you're legs up for this Donald Duck. Who gonna look pretty stupid. Pickin you up in his dump truck? In front of some gorgeous house in Rockaway.

FAY: Rockaway? What happened out there this time? You get your brain fried in Iran?

ROY: *Fuckin Iran! (He bangs table, rises, and paces away.)*

RITA: I was at the hostage parade. It was cold? But I was there.

MANFRED: A crime against the international conventions. *(To FAY)* He was in Iran how could that be?

FAY: Not Iran. Arabia. I dunno.

ROY: It don't! Matter. Where I was. What matters is.

(Looks at others; they nod expectantly)

ROY: Is. *(Beat; to FAY)* A guy died out there.

(Pause)

FAY: *(Confused)* A guy. Died?

ROY: On this trip, Fay. And I want. Some results. I want. Satisfaction.

FAY: What guy? How?

ROY: Stop askin questions! Just remember, I'm doin this for you!

FAY: Doin what??? *(Points at bottle)* You're parboiled. Take a nap. *(Turns to go)*

ROY: I say to you, fifty fat ones! Straight capital for a lucrative thing here of a car service. For a house. That you always said you wanted. With lawn furniture and a suckass patio—

FAY: *(Cutting him off)* Bogart wants to go to this disco on Northern Boulevard. So I'll be out til morning, Dad.

Cause I don't wanna hear from this fifty thousand
dollar question, O K? *(She turns to go; halts bristling at*
ROY's *next speech.)*

ROY: And she says, pardon me, I gotta go this disco
on cheezy Northern Boulevard. With this pineapple
pansy? Ain't got but a quarter to shove up a pinball
machine. But hey. I'll see *you.* And your fifty Gs? When
I get time. *(Waves)* Have a nice day. *(To* MANFRED*)* I
raised her. To be smarter. *(Sits)* Than this.

FAY: *(Whipping around)* You get fifty Gs. In your hand.
And we'll talk plan. But until you got money. Where
your big mouth opens—

(Quickly, overlapping:)

ROY: I gotta buy you?

FAY: And closes and opens then I am going—

ROY: I gotta buy your love?

FAY: With Bogart. To this disco. On Northern
Boulevard.

ROY: With hard cash?

FAY: *Hard somethin!*

(Beat)

ROY: You. Are some daughter.

FAY: Somethin real you can count it. Always with
Mommie you went. Hold on don't leave me I got this
plan. They got oil in Lebanese I know a guy. Or you
gonna soak a year's wages in some Gristede's in Egypt.
She would sit here—

ROY: I don't need this, Fay.

FAY: And drink and say. I married a poop.

ROY: Keep talkin.

FAY: I'm thirty years old my back aches and I am up to my yazoo in poop.

ROY: In six months you turn into this?

FAY: What I turned into, Dad. Was a woman. With a body and some brains!

(ROY *stares at* FAY.)

RITA: He's still your dad, Fay.

FAY: (*Softening a bit; to* ROY) You was fun I was little. You're a good guy. When you ain't drinkin and makin with the bullshit.

RITA: And your mother, Fay, was no charm bracelet.

FAY: I love you I never said different. You're funny, you're crazy, you're a stick of dynamite. But bullshit *hurts*, Dad! And I am not gonna sit here like Mommie starin at the walls and waitin for this plan.

RITA: Roy's day will come, Fay. Have faith.

ROY: (*Leaping up; exploding at* RITA) EAT! YOUR LIPS!

(RITA *turns away, hurt.*)

FAY: Stop! Yellin! (*Quiet*) At Rita.

(ROY *slowly sits, breathing hard, gripping and staring at bottle.*)

(*Silence*)

RITA: (*Sadly*) Manfred? We should go. This here is. Family.

MANFRED: Oh. Sure. So Roy. We come back tonight?

ROY: (*Looking up at* MANFRED; *calmer*) Sure.

MANFRED: (*Rising*) It's a big day here. I'll call my brother and set up your finance. Then we all come back after the block party and celebrate. You, me, Fay, and this kumquat. You *gotta* meet this kumquat, Roy.

(ROY *raises the bottle at* MANFRED *and nods.*)

(MANFRED *and* RITA *cross to entrance door,* RITA *squeezing* FAY'*s arm supportively.* RITA *pauses at door.*)

RITA: So we'll see you after the block party? We'll all come back and visit nice.

(RITA *and* MANFRED *exit.*)

(Beat)

ROY: *(To* FAY*)* O K. Fine. Your mother was your mother. She left, fine. For all I know. Or care? She's in Teaneck. O K? But you, Fay. You can have better. If you just— *(Gropes for words)*

FAY: Just what? Tell me.

ROY: Just— *(Angrily)* Stop messin with duckshit and gimme some support! I'm under a lotta pressure here. I got appointments. With lawyers and shit.

FAY: *(Suspiciously)* Lawyers?

ROY: We're talkin that kinna money we're talkin finance.

FAY: *(Approaching table; looking closely at* ROY*)* What's with the lawyers? Come on, Dad. What you mixed up in? This guy who died out there. And these lawyers. There's a connection here?

ROY: Yeah, there's a connection. You think I'm bullshit? Well, a guy died and his wife is suin the shipowner it's a big case. And I. Am very central to the whole thing. This lawyer is comin here today and what I want is this— *(Gropes again for words)*

FAY: Yeah?

ROY: Is for you to be here tonight and share my satisfaction. Not with that kotex, but alone. What I have to no through today is for you and I want some support I want my daughter.

FAY: You got me worried, Dad, all this with the big case. You're this A B. This is your life. Don't fuck it up.

ROY: A life? With O'Farrell Lines?

FAY: You got your pension you got your status don't fuck it up with this. This whatever with the dead guy and the lawyers.

ROY: Status? On cans fulla plantains and cheap mitty blouses outa Hong Kong? I ship out onna tanker I'm still toilet paper. Don't talk status at me.

FAY: You'll get your soch, you'll get your comp.

ROY: And die in Queens.

FAY: You live here. Why not die here?

ROY: *You* wanna die here? Or you wanna live a nice big house in Rockaway?

FAY: *(Contemptuously)* Rockaway?

ROY: Or wherever! How's it sound to you? Florida.

FAY: It's where Jews go. To eat sand and die.

ROY: So a house in Westchester

FAY: Westchester? How you gonna?

ROY: Gonna take that fifty Gs and buy into a car service with Manfred's brother the big shot. Then I'm gonna plop your ass in a limo, drive you up to like New Rochelle. And say to you. My daughter. Take your pick. Any house you want.

FAY: It's that easy?

ROY: You grab.

FAY: You what?

ROY: *(Clutching at air with fists)* You grab you grab you grab you grab! That's how it is. *(Looks at hands)* It's in the fingers the way they curl. You gotta be ready. *(Looks at FAY)* Fine. I'm ready. *(Looks again at hands)* I

got the bones in my fingers ready to bust out my tips.
(Silence. His hands are before him. Abruptly he drops them.)
And I want my daughter.

FAY: Don't do this, Dad.

ROY: You be here, Fay. Not with old Bo-Bo but alone.

FAY: Don't do this for me.

ROY: In my hand, Fay. There's gonna be. Not cash
money, maybe. But a check. Not for all of it, maybe.
But for some of it. And when you see it, in my
hand, you gonna know. That that house. In fuckin
Westchester? Is real.

FAY: I'll be here.

ROY: *(Elated)* Thank you, Fay. From the legs.

FAY: Oh, I'll be here. Like always. To hold your
forehead over the toilet. To pick up your broken pieces.
To watch you try to smile when your face hurts. I'll be
here.

(Beat, as ROY clenches his fists)

(FAY crosses upstage to entrance door and opens it.)

ROY: *This time, Fay, I'm a winner!*

(Exit FAY.)

(ROY crosses his arms and smiles defiance.)

*(Low tinkling carnival music floats softly through the open
window.)*

(Lights dim.)

END OF ACT ONE

ACT TWO

(That afternoon. Italian rock `n roll and festive voices, excited, intense, rise up from the street.)

(ROY, in his ill-fitting blue suit, hands in pockets, no tie, is standing by the window, staring down at the crowded street.)

(Buzzer. Music breaks off.)

(ROY abruptly spins about, looking nervously into room.)

(Buzzer again. ROY crosses to box, pushes button.)

ROY: *(Into box)* Yeah? *(Listens. Into box:)* Right. Third floor front.

(ROY hastily opens entrance door slightly, after leaning hard on buzzer. Goes to table, grabs bottle, puts it away under sink. Goes to daybed and quickly straightens covers. Notices duffel and leaps upon it, replacing its guts and then flinging it into closet. He must lean against closet door to get it shut.)

(A tentative knocking at door)

(ROY finally gets closet door to shut as PHILIP GAMBLE peeps around partially opened door.)

GAMBLE: Mr Bonino?

ROY: So. Hey.

(Beat, as GAMBLE and ROY stare)

ROY: I mean. Come in. It's open.

GAMBLE: Thank you. *(He slowly enters, in light summer suit, expensively tailored, carrying a briefcase. Looks around, smiling tentatively; closes door)*

ROY: So uh. You're the one onna phone yesterday?

GAMBLE: Yes. I'm Gamble, Philip Gamble.

ROY: Did you know I was callin alla way from Norfolk? It's where we always dock, then I bus it up here.

GAMBLE: Really? *(Mops forehead with handkerchief)* Extraordinary.

ROY: Hell, it's nothin. I call people from Norfolk alla time.

GAMBLE: *(Gesturing towards window)* Uh. I meant the block party.

ROY: Oh. That. Very ethnic this neighborhood. We got Italian we got Jew. Chink. You Jewish?

GAMBLE: Not all lawyers are Jewish, Mr Bonino.

(ROY nods. Awkward pause)

ROY: So hey. Come on in. You never been this neighborhood?

GAMBLE: No. *(He moves downstage to stand by table.)*

ROY: You know, that's a funny thing. You can be New York— You New York?

(GAMBLE carefully places briefcase on its side on table.)

GAMBLE: No.

ROY: Even if you was. You can live all your life New York and never leave your borough. My mother? Was strictly Queens. You told her Manhattan and it's like you said. Morocco.

GAMBLE: *(Smiling)* Yes. *(Drops smile)* You called yesterday on this Macayza case?

ROY: Sad thing.

GAMBLE: Is indeed.

ROY: A very sad thing.

GAMBLE: Yes.

ROY: You Manhattan? You look Manhattan.

GAMBLE: *(Smiling)* Only by day. I have a home in New Jersey.

ROY: So sit down.

GAMBLE: Oh. Thank you.

(GAMBLE sits at table; ROY remains standing.)

ROY: Got kids?

GAMBLE: What?

ROY: At home. In New Jersey.

GAMBLE: Yes. Two children. A boy and a girl.

ROY: How old?

GAMBLE: Three and five. My son is—

ROY: *(Cutting him off)* That's a good age. You wanna drink?

GAMBLE: *(Slight hesitation)* If you're. Having one.

ROY: Sure, why not? *(He moves upstage to kitchenette. As he does so:)* A good age it's not so good later. I got a daughter she's sixteen. *(Takes scotch bottle from under sink. Looks in fridge)* It's a wild age. Specially girls. *(Removes ginger ale, close fridge)* It's hard on fathers. *(Fixes drinks on counter)* In particular. When the father. Is a seaman. Get me?

GAMBLE: I'm sure it is. *(Takes out pencil; getting down to business)* Now—

ROY: *(Cutting him off)* You can't be around that much, you know what I'm sayin?

GAMBLE: Oh? *(Looking around)* Your wife doesn't—?

ROY: She uh. Left. I got a friend upstairs she comes down and checks it out, you know. But it's not the same thing.

GAMBLE: Oh

ROY: And clothes. Jesus, you know the cost a girl's clothes these days?

GAMBLE: Yes, I—

ROY: Modelling.

GAMBLE: What?

ROY: Also she wants to take modelling. It hard. And you know. What a seaman makes. *(He crosses to table with drinks. Stands with drinks in hand, smiling at* GAMBLE*)* Not like a lawyer. Now a lawyer makes plenny.

GAMBLE: *(Smiling)* Not as much as your think.

ROY: Sure. It's tough today. And you hadda go to school for this.

GAMBLE: Exactly.

ROY: *(Not moving a muscle)* Here it is.

GAMBLE: What?

ROY: *(Slowly extending glass)* Your drink.

GAMBLE: *(Not taking it; unsnapping briefcase)* Thank you, but could I have some ice in that? *(Carefully removes a folder from briefcase)* I'm overheated. Quite a trek out here.

ROY: Rocks it is. *(He puts one glass on table, takes other to kitchenette. As he does so:)* You cab it?

GAMBLE: Yes.

*(*ROY *opens fridge, begins struggling with impacted ice tray.)*

ROY: Nice, you get to do that. Me, I go to Manhattan I gotta take the B M T transfer Queens Plaza.

GAMBLE: I'd get lost I'm sure.

(As ROY *struggles with ice tray,* GAMBLE *surreptitiously lifts lid of briefcase.)*

ROY: *(Struggling)* Shit!

(GAMBLE *carefully turns on a tape recording device inside briefcase)*

GAMBLE: I hope it's no trouble.

ROY: *(Same)* Fuck no. *(Yanks tray from fridge)* God damn!

(GAMBLE *delicately lowers lid of briefcase as* ROY *noisily clatters tray into sink)*

ROY: *The mayor!*

GAMBLE: *(Startled)* I beg your—?

ROY: The fuckin mayor says the cars? Are air-condition. *(Hacks at ice tray with utensil)* Bullshit! You are ridin a steambath into Manhattan! *(Finally cracks ice)* Fuck the mayor! *(Empties out tray and flings it into sink)* Fuck him! Run the A-train straight up his tubes! *(He stares into sink. Turns, looks at* GAMBLE*)* You get my meaning?

GAMBLE: *(Nervously)* I. Yes.

*(*ROY *plops cubes into glass.)*

ROY: Onna rocks. *(He crosses to table, hands* GAMBLE *his drink. Gestures at folder)* You gonna take notes?

GAMBLE: *(Gesturing with pencil, explanatory)* Well, my client, you see—

ROY: You unnerstand I can't sign nothin?

GAMBLE: Oh no. Just to keep it all straight. For my client.

ROY: You mean O'Farrell Lines?

GAMBLE: Right. As you know, Mr Bonino—. Its *Roy* Bonino, isn't it?

ROY: That's it.

GAMBLE: I'm Phil Gamble, the attorney for O'Farrell Lines. That is, *we* are—Burnham, Finster & Burke...

ROY: Hey. We been through all that.

GAMBLE: Just, Mr Bonino, to keep it straight. And I came out here this afternoon because you phoned me yesterday wanting to know...what O'Farrell might...*do* for you if you testified for them in this Macayza case. That is, instead of...for the other side. Correct?

ROY: You pretty young to be a lawyer.

GAMBLE: *(Strained smile)* Well, I'm just starting out. *(Resuming, businesslike)* So was that the substance of your—

ROY: You got the house payments.

GAMBLE: Yes.

ROY: And the kids. And your wife has to look good, right?

GAMBLE: Well, she tries—

ROY: It ain't so cheap in New Jersey. I mean, where it's nice New Jersey.

GAMBLE: Certainly isn't.

ROY: But you doin O K. Startin out a big Manhattan law firm.

GAMBLE: It's not all that big, Mr Bonino, and maritime law is not the most lucrative nor is it—

ROY: But you doin O K. It's a start.

GAMBLE: Yes.

ROY: And this is a big case. Could make you.

GAMBLE: Well, we've lots of cases.

ROY: How much is that—that Mac—Mac—

GAMBLE: Macayza.

ROY: Yeah. We called him Jesus. *(English pronunciation)*
How much that Macayza's wife suin you for?

GAMBLE: *(Offhand)* Oh. She. It's about. Five million.

ROY: It's a big case.

GAMBLE: Well, they don't expect to get it. Its just a
figure.

ROY: Even so.

GAMBLE: Well—

ROY: Even. So. *(Lowers voice)* You pull it off and
O'Farrell. Gotta be very. Grateful.

GAMBLE: *(Cupping his ear)* What way that? I'm sorry.

ROY: *(Normal voice)* It's important. A man died out
there. A young Spanol? With a wife and a shitload of
kids? And O'Farrell Lines, is it responsible? This! Is the
long and the short.

*(Raises his glass to GAMBLE; the lawyer quickly responds in
kind. They drink, and ROY sits across table from GAMBLE.)*

GAMBLE: Mr Bonino, I'm wondering. Did you talk with
Mr Isaacson?

ROY: The lawyer for the wife? Yes, I did.

GAMBLE: And is Mr Isaacson offering you anything for
your testimony?

ROY: He might of. He might of. He might of and he
might of not. O K? I mean, you're askin me somethin
that is my affair.

GAMBLE: So what am I dealing with here? So far as the.
Proposals go. If Isaacson's offering you a day's wages,
then we can offer you that also.

ROY: *(Glum)* A day's wages.

GAMBLE: That you would get if you were on a ship. A day's wages and expenses. That the *lawful* procedure for taking someone's testimony.

ROY: *(Drinks)* Expenses?

GAMBLE: Well, for instance, if someone is coming in from out of town to testify, then we pay his expenses. Transportation costs, if necessary a hotel. Of course, you being in the city—

ROY: We're talkin a subway token.

GAMBLE: Well, tell me what type of area I'm dealing in. So I can relay it to my client.

ROY: Be fair, that's all! Cause I don't go for this pay stuff. This carfare. Cause you know, we seamen don't get paid much money. You know, we only get paid forty, fifty dollars a day, somethin like that. Hell, I wouldn't go from here to across the street for that. I guess you unnerstand.

GAMBLE: Well, I deal with witnesses a lot and they do it all the time. That is, I pay them their daily wages and expenses.

ROY: You might be dealin with these Puerto Ricans and shit, but you know I'm no Puerto Rican.

GAMBLE: I deal with all sorts of people.

ROY: When you got a good case, maybe you offer this.

GAMBLE: Why, I think we have a very good case here.

ROY: *(Leaning forward)* No. You don't. *(Beat, as he drinks)*

GAMBLE: What, Mr Bonino, exactly what do you mean?

ROY: I mean to say that you never know. About a guy like Jesus. Or about a hatch ladder.

(Beat. GAMBLE chews end of pencil.)

ROY: A thing like this? A case this big? Could go either way.

GAMBLE: Our way. Or Isaacson's way?

ROY: There you go.

GAMBLE: So if I indicate to you. That I want it to go *our* way. Then you'd testify along those lines?

ROY: You're learnin somethin here.

GAMBLE: And of course, for this service, we have to make it worth your while?

ROY: That is very true. I mean, would *you* go into court dance around for carfare? They don't pay you good, you don't show up, right?

GAMBLE: *(Coldly)* I really don't know.

ROY: *(Waves hand, indicating apartment)* Look, I plead my situation and it's damn hard here. You live in a place this small? With the landlord he never paints it? You can't afford to fix your air condition? You got a sixteen year-old daughter steamin up the place? *(Leans across table) Treatin you like shit!*

(GAMBLE stares.)

ROY: I bet nobody ever treated you like shit. In your whole life. *(He drinks, then smiles at* GAMBLE.*)* So how you doin?

GAMBLE: *(Nervous)* Fine.

ROY: So you see how it is.

GAMBLE: Yes.

ROY: So. How you doin?

GAMBLE: Fine. Now, what if—. How about if we paid you the overtime rate?

ROY: *(Glum)* Fifteen bucks an hour.

GAMBLE: Well. Whatever. It is.

ROY: *(Calm, ominous, examining his drink)* You come around here, you better be talkin. Fifty. Thousand. Smacks.

GAMBLE: Ah.

ROY: You know what I think? They drink that for lunch. Perks. I heard. Those big corporations.

GAMBLE: Yes, well. But for that my client would expect—

ROY: Important. Information.

(Drains glass)

*(*GAMBLE *nods.* ROY *crosses to kitchen counter and the scotch bottle)*

GAMBLE: You mentioned something about Mr Macayza and the hatch ladder.

ROY: *(Pouring drink)* I did? Yeah well. What I meant was that Macayza. Jesus and I. Was acquaintances.

GAMBLE: Friends.

ROY: I wouldn't say friends. I'd say acquaintances. We met ourself aboard ship different times. You know, couple two times.

GAMBLE: I see. And—?

ROY: I didn't know him all that well. Only we'd, you know. Now and then. We knock back a few. *(Lifts glass at* GAMBLE, *drinks)* Jesus was… *(Smiles, slouching at counter)* Hey.

GAMBLE: Sir?

ROY: You magine namin your kid Jesus? These Spanish. No Italian do that. Name his kid Christ. Hey, Christ, its your bedtime. Or. Christ, you little snot, drink your milk. *(Laughs)*

GAMBLE: So you were acquaintances. Went out, had drinks together?

ROY: Yeah. Like in Aden.

GAMBLE: The port where it happened?

ROY: That Jesus. A funny kid. Good shipmate, but you know, young, cocky.

GAMBLE: How so?

ROY: I'll be very frank with you.

GAMBLE: I'd appreciate it. *(Cupping ear)* And could you speak up? The street noise.

ROY: *(Louder)* In fact, he boarded the ship in Philadelphia and if you study his history now, he has a reputation of gettin on ships and gettin off ships and he always got a beef.

GAMBLE: Yes, we understand he made several claims against other companies. And you say that Macayza was known for making more or less *unfounded* claims? Well, I guess some guys make a living at that. They claim they hurt themselves and they really don't?

ROY: Cause I mean, I been sailin many years and we all know these guys. Now Jesus? He's noted for it.

GAMBLE: Really? I didn't know that.

ROY: There's a lot you don't know.

GAMBLE: Well, lets face it. There's some things only you seamen know. Such as how some guys claim, you know, they make up a claim that they hurt themselves. And later bring suit against the shipowner.

ROY: And you guys settle.

GAMBLE: Sometimes, yes. It's less trouble to pay out a portion of the claim. It's hard getting evidence months later, finding witnesses.

ROY: Cause seamen. Won't blow the cover. On other seamen. *(Smiling, he crosses to table and sits.)* You don't drink a whole lot?

GAMBLE: No. A cocktail now and then. At lunch.

ROY: Perks.

GAMBLE: Mr Bonino, fifty thousand dollars is a lot of information.

ROY: *(Expansive; rising and sauntering about)* O K. So you get into port and you go out with this acquaintance, don't matter who. You go out and pop a couple. And you get to talkin. And feelin pretty good. For the first time in a month or more, you're feeling pret. Ty. Good. And you start talkin about this and that and that and then you mention. Just you know casual. About this hatch ladder. Kinda shaky, you wouldn't notice. But shaky. Might be dangerous. And you're laughin and this and let's say you're this P R who gets a little cocky. You know how they are. Eat shit for months and then all of a sudden like... *(Cups hand over crotch)* You feature? Gotta show a little. Show how you're dick up. How actually you're on top. Get me?

(GAMBLE nods.)

ROY: You don't need a map on this?

(GAMBLE shakes his head.)

ROY: Tells how a guy could tear off a piece with this shaky hatch ladder. Hurt himself a little. Not bad. And collect. So what do you call that?

GAMBLE: Call what?

ROY: When a guy let's say a P R. Can't hold his juice and gets it into his head to go back and fuck around with this ladder, maybe bust his ankle some shit. And he goes back to the tub and it's late and dark and he's looped like a spic and. And he falls. *(Passes hand across face)* And falls. What do you call that?

(Beat)

GAMBLE: Contributory negligence. With intent.

ROY: Yeah, there'd be a lotta that, right?

GAMBLE: Right. Did you. Afterwards. After drinking and so on. Did you accompany Mr Macayza back to the ship?

ROY: Hey. *(Sitting at table again)* This is like for instance.

GAMBLE: I see.

ROY: Like. What if.

GAMBLE: How much, Mr Bonino, how much of this have you told Mr Isaacson?

ROY: That is my affair. But I will say this. I am givin you first grabs. Cause I figure it's worth more to you than to him.

GAMBLE: How do you figure that?

ROY: Cause without it? Without this for instance? This maybe if? You got a shaky ladder and a dead seaman.

GAMBLE: That's all very interesting, you know, because we've had no report of a shaky hatch ladder.

ROY: This does not surprise me.

GAMBLE: Well, of course we haven't boarded her yet. To investigate. Was it the forward hatch?

ROY: *(Leaning forward)* This does not. Surprise me.

GAMBLE: It doesn't?

ROY: *(Holding up two fingers, twining them)* The chief mate and the bosun? Like that.

GAMBLE: You mean. Some officers. After the accident. Secured the ladder without telling anyone? Without reporting that it was defective?

ROY: A few repairs. Late at night. It's no big deal.

GAMBLE: A cover-up. A *provable* cover-up.

ROY: A guy might of noticed a few things. A guy hangin round late.

GAMBLE: I see.

ROY: Cause like I told you, I have this daughter here, and a whole bunch of expenses and all that stuff. And I can't afford to stay onna beach. What I call the beach is on land, get me?

GAMBLE: Sure.

ROY: Alla time I gotta scramble for a berth. But I wanna spend more time here. With my daughter she needs me.

GAMBLE: Mr Bonino, about this ladder—

ROY: How old you say your daughter was?

GAMBLE: Uh. Five.

ROY: That's a good age. But it ain't the same as sixteen. She can look back and say she had lots of time. Your daughter. With her daddy. But with me my daughter never had this. Fay. My daughter. She never had this with me.

GAMBLE: I understand. Of course.

ROY: No, I don't think you do. It's different, you and me. Like different planets. *(Rises from table)* Come with me.

GAMBLE: What?

(ROY crosses to bedroom; as he does so:)

ROY: Come in here, counselor.

(ROY exits into bedroom. Beat, as GAMBLE hesitates, shakes his head, puts down pencil, rises and follows, to stand in bedroom doorway. Parts beaded curtain and observes ROY)

ROY: Look at this. This here's a one-bedroom apartment. I sleep in the daybed out there so's my daughter she's sixteen can have some privacy. You share a one-bedroom with your little girl? And this stuff she picks up! *(Grabs Snoopy pillow, throws it*

down.) See, I never bought her nothin. Little things,
sure, but no nice beautiful soft things. She's a pretty
girl, counselor. She usta be a good girl. I can't *give* her
nothin. I can't stop her from slippin away into that
ugly hole out. there—

GAMBLE: *(Sympathetic)* Mr Bonino, I understand.

ROY: You do?

GAMBLE: You need money.

ROY: *I need somethin beautiful, asshole!*

(Pushes GAMBLE *aside, exits bedroom, crosses to table, sits,
drains glass, slams it down)*

ROY: Jesus, you got to go to college and they teach you
all that negligence and whatever. But they don't teach
you. About guys like me.

GAMBLE: *(Nodding, returning to table)* I'm confused.
About a few things.

ROY: *(Nodding hack at him)* Right. They don't teach you
about—

GAMBLE: *(Taking up pencil.)* Such as. About the ladder.

ROY: *(Glumly)* The ladder.

GAMBLE: And exactly who secured it. And when that
was…

ROY: This is not the thing, my man.

GAMBLE: And whether you were with Mr Macayza
when—

ROY: *This is not the thing!* (Beat, quiet) That I'm talkin.
See?

GAMBLE: Mr Bonino, this will all have to come out in a
court of law. Don't *you* see that?

ROY: Court a law.

GAMBLE: Yes, I'm afraid so.

ROY: You heard all that I said?

GAMBLE: Yes.

ROY: So O K! I come up to your office, we hit that courtroom. For a price, you follow'? I will leave out this with the bosun. Go what you do is you cut me, now, a check on account. So I know you're serious on this. See, my daughter is comin here, and I wanna have somethin to *show* her.

GAMBLE: In a court of law you'll have to tell it all, Mr Bonino. The whole and exact truth. Regardless of— your daughter.

(Beat)

ROY: So hey. I can tell it this way for you or I can tell it the other way for Isaacson.

GAMBLE: You can't do that, Mr Bonino. It's perjury. *(Softening)* Look. What counts in law—

ROY: What counts is *this*! *(Rises, paces away, turns back, away)* That you take a seaman some *stupid*. Some guy he can't even speak English some *nigger*! He gets hurt and you put him onna stand and you make him look like this shithead! You twist him up you twist him down finally you say. Hey. Here's ten bucks. Take it. You slipped onna icy deck cause O'Farrell didn't put nothin down? Too bad. Says here you slipped two years ago. You slip an awful lot, don't you? You this miscontent or some shit? So take the ten bucks. Seamen know, buddy boy, we know what you do. You say this and this and you confuse us and you say, hey. You ever take a drink? Sure, I take a drink I'm fuckin crazy with this tub. O K, you took a drink you cracked your head onna coaming that's this contributory. Take the ten bucks, niggerhead. And *this*! *(Jabbing finger at* GAMBLE*)* Is the whole and exact truth. *This*! Is how you make your livin.

(Pause)

GAMBLE: Mr Bonino, I have the greatest respect for seamen and their problems.

ROY: What you, you're a company lawyer. You ever defend a seaman?

GAMBLE: No. However—

ROY: You think I'm some retard, but I know you!

GAMBLE: I can only reiterate, Mr Bonino, that I sympathize with seamen's problems.

ROY: This ain't no Spanol here. No nickel-dime seaman here.

GAMBLE: The law is the law, Mr Bonino.

ROY: The law is a two-twatted hooker, you want my estimation! I mean, *you!* You wanner tear off a piece? You go to these lunches get these perks go into court tear your piece right off. It's all part of the thing it's respectable. But me? You just look at my record those are good records! I never had myself not one speck of trouble. But *I* wanna piece? I gotta get dirty. Cheap and. Dirty. *This!* Is the law.

GAMBLE: Mr Bonino, this all is, isn't it, beside the point?

ROY: Oh, I see the point. It's stickin outa your face! And it says. *(Leaning forward)* There's this whore sittin at my table. Tellin me the territory is staked.

GAMBLE: *(Coldly repeats)* Whore.

ROY: Hey. Don't offense on this. I could be the whore, too.

GAMBLE: Mr Bonino, let me be sure I have all this.

ROY: Sure. From one whore to another whore.

GAMBLE: Don't push me, Mr Bonino.

ROY: Cut the crap, sonny boy! You just write down what I said. *(Yanks pencil from* GAMBLE's *grasp, then thrusts it back at him)* You write it down take it back to O'Farrell some grown-up man over there will be innerested.

GAMBLE: *(Taking pencil)* I will certainly relay your proposal to my client. *(Begins tapping pencil on folder)* But before I do, I think I should make a few things clear. I am an attorney. A reputable attorney. And any reputable attorney knows that you cannot go around buying testimony. Especially. *(Stops tapping)* From a seaman. A confused. Unhappy. Bitter. Drunken. Seaman.

(Silence. GAMBLE *lifts lid of briefcase, places folder inside. Shuts briefcase)*

ROY: *(Watching him)* You got a lotta vomit. To sit here and say this. In my face. To me.

GAMBLE: *(Rising from chair)* I will relay your proposal, Mr Bonino.

ROY: And you tell 'em to cut me a check today and get it over here! Cause if they don't? Isaacson and me gonna have their asses!

GAMBLE: Good-bye, Mr Bonino. *(He crosses to entrance door.)*

ROY: *(Leaping to his feet)* I know you! If I ever bit it? You would come in here! And say to my daughter. *Here's ten dollars for your dead daddy!*

*(*GAMBLE *stiffens; opens door, exits.)*

*(*ROY *grabs bottle and toasts the retreating figure. then drinks from it, deeply.)*

(Through the window, carnival sounds and laughter. Lights dim)

END OF ACT TWO

ACT THREE

(That night. Stage is dim. Scotch bottle is standing empty on table in central room. Phone, off the hook, is also on table.)

(Street music and a lurid carnival light pour in through the open window. The music is now discordant, tired, jangled, surreal. Occasional broken voices.)

(ROY, unconscious, in undershirt and wrinkled blue slacks, is lying on FAY's bed in the bedroom, one arm extended over the end of the bed, his body curled around the Snoopy pillow.)

(A knock at the door. RITA's voice is heard offstage, from the landing.)

RITA: *(Singsong)* BO-NIIII-NO!

(ROY does not stir. A louder knocking. He jerks awake. MANFRED's voice is also heard offstage.)

MANFRED: Roy! You missed the block party! It sucked!

(ROY turns over with a groan, falls off the bed. Rises, stands, stumbles into vanity, stares into mirror, as the following loud, drunken communication takes place on the landing:)

RITA: *(To MANFRED)* It was not no suck. You lost your kumquat so what? *(Singsong again)* BO-NIIII-NO!

MANFRED: *(To RITA)* The fuck are you? Lost nothin, I *rejected* the bitch!

RITA: Sam Indelicato? Was how you rejected her!

MANFRED: She wants Indelicato she can have Indelicato!

RITA: I would take him. *(Calling)* ROY???

(ROY stumbles into bathroom.)

MANFRED: *(To RITA)* Indelicato wouldn't touch you. He's a teamster.

RITA: What do you mean, he wouldn't? He touched your kumquat! And that kumquat, Manfred, was a linguini!

MANFRED: So what do you want from a teamster???

RITA: *(Calling)* Roy??? You gonna let us in? *(She rattles door; it opens.)* It's open!

(RITA and MANFRED enter drunkenly, he waving unopened scotch bottle. They look around. RITA giggles.)

RITA: She had no boobies and thighs like—

MANFRED: *(Appropriate hand motion)* Menza-menza. She was menza-menza. *(Meaning "So-So")*

RITA: Like linguini. *(Poking about room)* Where's Roy?

MANFRED: She was a type, that's all.

RITA: She was knockin people over with those thighs.

(ROY emerges from bathroom into bedroom, towelling his face.)

MANFRED: *(To RITA)* I ain't gonna stand here! In this apartment! Talkin! To some jealous spit!

RITA: You should die in your sleep I'm jealous!

(ROY strides out of the bedroom.)

MANFRED: Roy!

RITA: Roy honey. *(Opening arms, cloying)* Happy summer.

(ROY *grabs* RITA *about the waist, twirls her about; she shrieks with glee.*)

ROY: Let's dance!

MANFRED: A real party! *(Holds up bottle; sets it on table)* Refreshment!

(MANFRED *watches delightedly as* ROY, *singing "That's Amore", spins* RITA *around and around, also to her delight.*)

RITA: Roy! You're dancin me to death!

MANFRED: The sailor home from the hill!

ROY: Fay likes to dance? So her old man's a dancer!

(ROY *spins* RITA *into a chair, then reaches for* MANFRED's *bottle.*)

ROY: Let's drink to my daughter!

RITA: *(Breathless)* Roy, where was you it was a lovely fair.

ROY: *(Playing caliope with empty and full bottles)* Havin my own block party!

MANFRED: *(Gesturing towards window)* Yeah, well that one's still goin on, and it sucks.

RITA: *(To* MANFRED) Suck. Suck. So what does that mean?

MANFRED: It means what it says!

ROY: *(Singing, playing with bottles)* "The moon inna sky—"

RITA: *(To* MANFRED) You always say this it's stupid.

ROY: *(Same)* "Is a big pizza pie—"

MANFRED: *(To* RITA) I know what it means!

ROY: "That's amore!"

RITA: *(Replacing phone on receiver; moving it elsewhere)* Roy, your phone is off the hook what if there was a fire?

ROY: There was a fire and I put it out! *(Grabs* RITA *around waist)* Let's start another one!

RITA: Roy! Eat somethin!

(A blast of discordant street music as ROY *spins* RITA *madly about room)*

RITA: Manfred! Go get a Sicilian!

MANFRED: *(Swaying on feet, not moving)* Sure.

*(*ROY *and* RITA *collapse in a heap on floor.)*

RITA: *(Breathless)* You need a slice, Roy. Cheese is good for your stomach, coats your lining.

ROY: My lining is steel-plated cast iron aluminum! Get up!

*(*RITA *giggles and they stagger to feet;* ROY *pinches her butt; she screeches with delight.)*

MANFRED: *(Still swaying in one spot)* Rita? You want a Sicilian?

RITA: *(Embracing* ROY*)* God Roy, it's just like it usta be.

(Abruptly ROY *pushes* RITA *away and moves to table and sits.)*

ROY: So come on! What are we waitin I wanna drink. *(Indicating new bottle)* You brung me this so let's have it.

RITA: Oh, Roy. You're embarrassed! *(Grabs empty off of table, sways towards kitchenette)* Such a sweetheart I'll wash up some glasses.

MANFRED: *(Sitting at table, opening bottle; to* ROY*)* New York. Would be perfect. If it just would cool off at night I stink. *(Beat)* So how'd it go?

ROY: What go?

MANFRED: Your finance. I called my brother and even over the phone? When I says you got fifty Gs? I could hear his eyes light up.

(No response from ROY*)*

MANFRED: So it's all set up it's a magnificent opportunity, Roy.

ROY: Opportunity? Is my middle name!

MANFRED: It is.

ROY: Up the cadoonies I got opportunity!

MANFRED: You do.

ROY: It's a great country for finance!

MANFRED: Coast to coast!

ROY: I have laid down with the Statue of Liberty and played tetherball with her tits!

MANFRED: Good for you!

RITA: *(Fumbling at sink)* Roy, stop it that's dirty.

MANFRED: Only me? It ain't so great.

ROY: *(To* RITA*)* So will you bring over the glasses?

RITA: The Statue of Liberty is a national shrine, Roy.

ROY: *(Indicating bottle)* So we can have some of this?

RITA: Oh. Sure. *(Brings dripping glasses to table and sits)*

MANFRED: *(To* ROY*)* So anyways, I meet my kumquat.

*(*ROY *reaches for bottle, hastily pours himself a drink.)*

MANFRED: We're walkin up and down the block everybody's inna street it's beautiful.

*(*ROY *drinks thirstily.)*

MANFRED: Hey. Roy. Slow down.

RITA: Bonino. Not so fast.

ROY: *(Pouring another)* I got my house in Westchester let's celebrate. *(Drinks, peers at* MANFRED*)* So what *you* got, cousin'? *(Italo-American slang for "good buddy"; pronounced "koo-jine")* Where's this kumquat you promise me?

MANFRED: Shit, Roy, I even and went and bought her a *cannoli!*

RITA: Does straight to her hips. You should eat, Roy, I'll get you somethin.

*(*RITA *rises, staggers to kitchenette, prepares potato chips.)*

MANFRED: *(To* ROY*)* I try and get her onna ferris wheel and she's all giggles.

RITA: *(At counter)* She woulda broke it.

ROY: So where is she, Manfred?

MANFRED: I buy her a cappuchin' she gets a little cream on her lips I flick it off with my tongue. I mean, she was hot and I was happy. And *then!* We meet Rita. Sittin out front on her folding chair?

RITA: Oh, so now it's my fault?

MANFRED: That was when the tide turned, Rita.

RITA: It turned you should drop dead.

MANFRED: So we're standin around shootin the shit with Rita, *fuck!* I wish we woulda moved on. So we're standin there. Talkin to Rita. Chatter chitter chatter yadda. And who comes up? You know that Sam Indelicato, we played pool with him that time his mother just died? Big guy, a teamster, kinna stupid?

ROY: *Goomba!* *(Meaning: "Close associate, family")* Where. Is. *(Knocks back drink)* The kumquat???

RITA: Sam's a goodlookin guy.

MANFRED: A slab of beef. So he comes up and says, right in front of the girl, "Hi, Manfred, how's your poodles?" Well, you know, Roy.

RITA: *(Returning to table with chips; sits)* It was funny.

MANFRED: It was not funny.

RITA: It was funny.

MANFRED: It's not funny in front a guy's girlfriend! Roy, it's the reputation we're gettin. Us pet store guys. It's all this Manhattan bullshit with the doggie boutiques. Sam goes, "Can I bring in my pekinese will you fluff her up?" Like I run a beauty parlor for mutts like I was a *hairdresser!*

RITA: *(Munching)* It was a comedy masterpiece. *(Offers chips to ROY)* Roy honey?

ROY: *(Waving away chips; to MANFRED)* Now, don't tell me. He comes on to her.

MANFRED: Right in front of my teeth!

RITA: She was comin on to him. From a block away you could hear those thighs rubbin together.

ROY: So lemme guess! He takes her off, says they'll get you guys some gelati. Some chianti.

MANFRED: *(Glumly nodding)* In a paper cup.

ROY: *(Slapping table)* I knew it!

RITA: We never. Saw her. Again.

MANFRED: *(To ROY; drinking)* Can you believe it?

ROY: *(Hard)* Yeah. I believe it. *(Suddenly expansive)* Only you can meet a whole new kumquat, Manfred! When I throw my first garden party in Westchester!

MANFRED: That's great, Roy.

ROY: Gonna settle down at last. Float around on a rubber thingie in my swimming pool!

RITA: You givin up the sea, Roy?

ROY: Cept for a Criss-Craft, maybe.

RITA: That's nice.

MANFRED: It is. He seen the world and now he gonna settle down.

RITA: He been so many places. Iraq and Iran.

(ROY *explodes, banging table.*)

ROY: *FUCKIN IRAN!!!*

MANFRED: *(Also banging table)* An international outrage!!!

RITA: *(Trying to calm them)* I know I know. I was there. For the hostage parade.

ROY: *(To* MANFRED*; pointing at* RITA*)* This! Is how I mean. Unfortunately what we got here. Is a country. Fulla *losers*!

RITA: *(Drinking)* Those hostages was very brave.

ROY: Who would let another country. Fulla *niggers*! Treat us like that. And then! Throw a parade the fuck about it.

RITA: Don't say this, Roy.

MANFRED: Bonino for President!

ROY: They need a *cousin'* inna White House! Cause I been around.

MANFRED: *(Raising glass)* Been around the world around the block!

RITA: Long live the hostages!

ROY: Dick the hostages! And those Iran over there, runnin around monkey mouth chop off your fingers act like *dope addicts*!

RITA: Yeah? And what am I suppose to do about it?

MANFRED: So Roy. What's the answer?

ROY: It's a deep. Very deep. *Conspiracy!*

MANFRED: That it!

ROY: Of those niggers over there. And guys over here. That look cool and. Smooth. Guys that look and act. That move and. And. And who talk about the whole and exact—*truth!*

RITA: What?

ROY: A conspiracy.

MANFRED: *(Blurry)* Right.

ROY: *(To MANFRED)* I mean the smooth ones! The ones got lemonade for piss got nice underarms! They got truth! They got justice! Out in Forest Hills?

MANFRED: Yeah?

ROY: *THEY GOT TENNIS! (Beat, as he drinks. Low, contemptuous)* And you innocents. Throw this parade. *(Masturbation gestures)* Yankin on your wee-wees rattle about these hostages when. There's this. Conspiracy.

(Silence)

MANFRED: You been around the block, Roy.

RITA: Those hostages? *(Raises glass)* Should be decorated. *(Lowers glass; explodes)* And Indelicato is a hunk!

ROY: He's a loser, Rita! Take it from me.

RITA: No.

ROY: So he was lucky he got inna union. But the union says, spread your cheeks. And there's this Delicato. With his big pink buns. Crackin a smile! That's a loser.

RITA: That is a very crude picture, Roy.

MANFRED: *(Chortling)* But it works!

RITA: A hunk and a hero!

MANFRED: *(Disgustedly)* A hunk. Jesus, Rita.

RITA: It makes a difference. A man and a woman it's two foreign countries.

ROY: Bitches.

RITA: Don't start with that Roy.

ROY: *Bitches!*

RITA: I won't sit still for this.

ROY: So go home.

RITA: This is insults I won't listen.

(ROY abruptly rises, crosses to bedroom doorway, shouts into bedroom.)

ROY: I hate anybody! That got a hole between their legs!

RITA: Yeah, well, Indelicato's a hunk and I love him!

ROY: *(Returning to table; to* MANFRED*)* Can you deal with it? A hole between your fucking legs? What kinna shit is that?

RITA: And what would you do, Roy? If we didn't have this? Huh? What?

MANFRED: *(In one breath)* We would play bocce we would drink wine we would go the distance.

RITA: *(To* MANFRED*)* You! Would be lost. You always say this about the kumquats. Talk talk you'd have nothin to talk.

MANFRED: I talk. But I do. Too. Also I do.

RITA: What you do is talk. But Indelicato? He. Do.

MANFRED: Me. Too.

RITA: You. Poo!

ROY: *What is this, some kinna nursey rhyme???*

(Beat. They all drink.)

RITA: Manfred, you are a lost person.

MANFRED: I am right here. On this island of Queens in the state of New York.

RITA: It was different with me and Roy.

ROY: *(Drinking)* Oh, Jesus! Eat it, Rita.

RITA: You would come to me, Roy. When you hadda fight with that woman down here. I remember very well, Roy.

ROY: I ain't! Gonna lissen to this. Dance with me. Or die. *(He rises and crosses to daybed; sits, staring at floor and drinking.)*

RITA: *(Rising, swaying, looking at* ROY*)* Roy would come to me, Manfred. So mad he couldn't talk. Roy's wife had this tongue, you remember? Like a bottle opener. And Roy would come upstairs and not say a word even. Just squeeze his fists and stand. In the middle of my apartment. And look at the floor. And you know what I did?

MANFRED: Yeah, I know what you did.

RITA: *(Moving tipsily towards* ROY*)* No cannoli no ferris wheel no jokes or come-ons! Just Roy Bonino in my apartment not a word in our mouths. And when he would come to me, Manfred. When he did this. *(Standing before* ROY, *spreading arms)* And I would take his head at my breasts. I felt like. Warm water. Like a bath that would make his body. Glow.

(Silence)

MANFRED: *(Giggling)* Like a bathtub.

*(*ROY *rises, returns to stand by table)*

MANFRED: Hey. Roy. Like a bathtub.

RITA: *(Swaying back to table; sitting)* You are a suck, Manfred.

(ROY *carefully sets down glass on table. Stares at it)*

ROY: *(Quietly)* Everybody this apartment. *(Exploding, sweeping bowl of chips onto floor) Is a loser!*

MANFRED: *(Placating)* But not you, Roy.

ROY: Oh no?

RITA: Were all losers!

MANFRED: *(To* RITA*)* So who asked you?

ROY: Gimme that! *(Grabs up bottle, chugalugs)*

RITA: Roy!

(MANFRED *rises and loosens bottle from* ROY'*s grasp, and gets him to sit.)*

MANFRED: Jesus, Roy, take it easy. Come on, sit down, *goomba.*

(ROY *gasps in his chair, looking away.)*

MANFRED: Shit Roy, it don't matter. Look at me, I been alone since my brother got married and moved to Hempstead. *(To* RITA, *as he sits)* It's very nice out there.

RITA: *(Blurrily)* I love Floral Park.

ROY: I want my Fay.

MANFRED: I said it don't matter. I score I don't score. I got my shop. I come over here I drink. Or I don't. Or I play pool. Now and then some girl. Comes inna shop maybe, or-maybe she's somebody's sister's girlfriend. Usually she's fat, I dunno, it's O K with me. Puts her fat legs around me. Must look pretty funny, hey? Afterwards she pats me on my butt. I got this funny butt they always tell me how funny. One girl, she tells me, Your butt is like a prune. Your butt. Is like…I never see her again. I would, only. I never. See her. *(Gestures helplessly; laughs)* So it don't matter!

(Silence. They drink.)

ROY: I love you, Manfred, old buddy. But it's a red-tag sale day today. At Korvettes. They're sellin ducks.

MANFRED: *(Blurrily; to* RITA*)* Korvettes?

RITA: He means. I dunno.

ROY: *(Raising glass)* To the losers! To Manduck and Rita Duck and Duck Bonino!

RITA: *(Also raising glass)* I'll drink to that!

MANFRED: Don't be depressing. I won't go to movies anymore they're too depressing.

RITA: You don't like depressing you don't like life!

ROY: That, Rita—

MANFRED: I just wanna be happy that's all I ask.

RITA: You're afraid to suffer? So get out!

ROY: I love you, too, Rita! *(He noisily scoots chair to her side, throws arm around her shoulder)* You know, Rita. You're ninety percent of the time. Banana head. But ten percent? Is sterling silver plated.

RITA: *(Touched)* Thank you, Roy.

*(*ROY *wetly kisses* RITA*'s cheek.)*

MANFRED: This is depressing.

RITA: *(Looking at* ROY *lovingly)* I miss you, Roy. Bad.

*(*ROY *and* RITA *kiss on the lips, long and sloppily, swaying between the chairs.)*

MANFRED: This is very very depressing.

*(*ROY *and* RITA *cease kissing, sway in an embrace.)*

RITA: *(Gasping, into* ROY*'s neck)* You never. Come to me. No more.

ROY: No, Rita.

RITA: *(Tears)* Why, Roy?

MANFRED: So what am I, a peep?

ROY: Don't need a woman, Rita.

RITA: You're a man. You're sad. A woman is *for* that.

ROY: I'm bullshit, Rita. *(He disentangles himself, lurches to his feet.)* A red-tag day'

(ROY drains glass, crosses in front of table, stumbles into MANFRED's chair; MANFRED steadies him.)

MANFRED: Roy baby. Get your sea legs.

(ROY pushes away from MANFRED, crosses to window, looks out.)

(A blast of twisted street music, swells, fades.)

RITA: Roy, you ain't bullshit and never was.

ROY: Always, Rita.

MANFRED: Roy, don't worry. You seen your lawyer, right?

ROY: I seen one. Later I talked to another onna phone.

MANFRED: Two lawyers? Rita, did I tell you? This is finance.

ROY: And you know what the second lawyer tells me?

MANFRED: The first one, Roy. *(Counts drunkenly on fingers)* Do it in order. Tell me what the first one said, and then what—

ROY: Shut-up, Manfred!

MANFRED: *(Angrily)* Roy. You and me we usta have. Simpatico. Now we got. You shit on me. What happened this trip you should shit on me?

ROY: Manfred, I'm tellin you what happened today!

MANFRED: *(Dully)* Sure.

ROY: So the second lawyer, name is Jew Isaacson? He calls me and says he heard from the first one, the one who was up here? That snotnose white boy?

MANFRED: Sure. The first one heard. From the second one. Fine.

RITA: *(To MANFRED, watching ROY)* Let him talk!

ROY: And Isaacson says, Why'd you tell Gamble all that about Jesus? Why didn't you just stay out of it, sailor? What about Mrs Macayza and her four kids? Ain't there some kinna fuckin code of the sea or some fuckin thing you would dump on your shipmate's family like this? *(Turning from window)* Can you deal with it?

RITA: I dunno, Roy.

MANFRED: The code of the sea. Now *that!* Is romantic.

RITA: If you own a pet shop, *anything* is romantic

MANFRED: The romance of the sea is a special thing women are not invited!

ROY: *Lissen to me!* First I got that snotnose today tellin me the law. And then, see, what I got, I got this jewey shyster yackin to me about a code! I ain't no prickface backstab of a fuckin traitor to some lowlife P R niggerhead what took his chances and fucked himself dead! *(Appealing to MANFRED and RITA)* What about the bosun and the mate? They got a code when they fix that ladder? I seen 'em do it! Or O'Farrell, it got a code when it bites off a seaman and spits out his bones? Everybody's onna grab!

MANFRED: *(Musing)* A girl in every port.

ROY: So I says to Isaacson, don't gimme no lectures! If Gamble don't wanna play, then *you* make me an offer! Gamble can't prove nothin!

MANFRED: A port in every country.

RITA: Roy, you in trouble?

ROY: And Issacson says. *(Beat)* He taped it, sailor! *(Beat; quiet:)* This whole thing is blown. They can supoena that tape. Mrs Macayza and her four kids? Gonna haveta settle outa court for catshit. But you, Bonino. The only thing you gonna get is your ass. *Blacklisted!* With the union. You won't never. Ever! Ship out again. So good-bye. *(Beat)* Sailor.

MANFRED: *(Still musing)* Life on the bounding main.

RITA: Somebody gonna fire you, Roy?

(ROY raises hands, helplessly.)

RITA: Roy, you're in trouble.

(RITA staggers across room to ROY.)

RITA: Roy. My Roy.

(RITA tries to embrace ROY.)

ROY: *(Shrugging her off)* Get away Rita. I gotta face my daughter.

RITA: *(Reaching out to him)* Baby, you gotta let go. You gotta hold somebody!

ROY: I want my daughter!

RITA: *(Clutching him)* Fay's a woman now, Roy. Let her go.

ROY: Shut up!

(ROY strikes RITA full in the face. She staggers backwards, stunned.)

(She sinks onto daybed.)

ROY: A red-tag day! *(He stumbles back to window, looks out.)* This ugly little block. With Christmas lights.

MANFRED: *(Blearily focussing on RITA)* Rita? You O K?

(RITA puts her hands to her face. Turns over on daybed. Passes out)

MANFRED: Roy. You didn't get the money.

(No response)

MANFRED: O K. Now my brother? He's a businessman and will understand. So don't worry *about* it.

ROY: *(Spinning round)* Fuck your brother! I don't got the Gs, I ain't got a job, me and my daughter gonna be on the street, and *you* say. Don't worry *about* it.

MANFRED: You're sellin yourself short.

ROY: This is forty-odd years old and how'm I gonna live?

MANFRED: Drink up.

(ROY slowly sits and they drink.)

ROY: Gotta face my daughter, Manfred. I promise her Westchester and she gets. The sidewalk.

MANFRED: It's just finance, Roy. Tell Fay. It's finance. That's what it is. She's your little girl. *(Lurches to feet)* This is the tie that binds, Roy. *(Crosses staggering to daybed)* Gotta sleep. *(Sinks down onto daybed. Laughing bitterly)* Boy. You shoulder seen that kumquat. *(Slumps next to RITA)*

RITA: *(Rising up, dreamily)* Indelicato?

MANFRED: *(Disgusted)* Suck the big one, Rita.

(They pass out, MANFRED's head at RITA's feet.)

(ROY stares before him as lights dim. Tired strains of distorted street music drift in through the open window. The reddish fair lights glow.)

(A rattling of entrance door. Music out, lights slightly up. Peeps in FAY)

FAY: Dad?

(ROY continues staring before him.)

(BOGART looks in over FAY's shoulder. She shakes her head at him, and pushes him back onto landing. Gestures for him to wait)

(Leaving door ajar, she moves on tiptoe into room, carrying her Danskin bag. Surveys scene, shaking her head)

FAY: This the big celebration?

ROY: You alone, Fay?

FAY: *(Looking over shoulder)* Yeah.

ROY: *(Squaring his shoulders)* Gotta tell you somethin, Fay.

FAY: What happened with the lawyers?

ROY: Got somethin to say to you, Fay.

FAY: I'm listening.

ROY: Just remember, Fay. Whatever happens. Your daddy, Always loves you. *(He falls forward, collapsing onto table.)*

(FAY stares, then approaches ROY. Tenderly she strokes his hair.)

(BOGART tentatively enters. Closing door, he moves downstage, a bottle paper-sacked in his hand.)

BOGART: So is it safe or what? So hey, I'm gonna stay tonight or what?

FAY: *(Stroking her father's head)* When he's this tanked he'll be out for days. You can leave early he'll never know.

BOGART: Why'd we come back so soon? We coulda got wasted, coulda got pissed in somebody's car.

FAY: I told you, My dad. He kept saying. Come back. Be here. *(Shrugs)* I dunno. Something about. Fifty thousand sheets.

(BOGART moves center stage, taking possession of the room, which he sweeps with his hand)

BOGART: Fifty thousand? At the corner of Futz and Turkey?

FAY: *(Bridling)* It was better maybe. At that disco you took me?

BOGART: Forget it. *(Turns towards bedroom)* Come on, I got a surprise for you.

FAY: *(Moving towards him)* The surprise, Bogart, is I spent my Saturday night. With fourteen hitters and a coupla mergatroids in blazers.

BOGART: *(Turning back to face her)* So I heard it was hot I'm sorry.

FAY: *(Starting for bedroom)* Looked like a football game at Queens College?

BOGART: Maybe you shoulda stayed home. With your dad.

FAY: *(Turning back to face him)* You been on this case. Of my dad. All night.

BOGART: Your dad. Listen. He woulda liked that disco.

(FAY and BOGART are nose to nose.)

FAY: From now on, you take me Manhattan.

BOGART: Manhattan is fulla bazoo and pink hair. And a cover.

FAY: So? It's my money.

BOGART: Yeah and so?

FAY: So get some of your own.

BOGART: I *said.* *(Unscrews cap of bottle in sack)* I got news here!

(BOGART starts to drink; FAY clutches at bottle; he holds on to it.)

FAY: You're no good to me shitface, Bogart.

BOGART: Don't worry about it, Fay.

FAY: I'm worried, Bogart.

BOGART: Well, don't bother, Fay.

FAY: I don't need, in my bed. Some kinna *slobber*! With arms and legs stickin out!

BOGART: You got a mouth on your face. And you know somethin? (*Yanks bottle away*) It's only good for one thing.

(FAY *crosses angrily into bedroom;* BOGART *follows. Lights up on bedroom*)

(*Lights down on central room. The reddish fair lights illuminate* ROY, *collapsed on table.*)

(FAY *has seated herself at vanity, unstrapping her shoes as* BOGART, *in doorway, watches her, nipping from bottle.*)

(*After a beat,* BOGART *enters bedroom.*)

BOGART: We need our own apartment, Fay.

FAY: You got security? Cash for the key?

BOGART: What I got is this good news for you, Fay. Only you went and ruint. The whole thing on me. Totally.

(FAY *ignores* BOGART.)

BOGART: Fay, I heard about a job.

(FAY *hesitates, then continues undressing, strewing clothes about.*)

FAY: What Job?

BOGART: I know this guy.

FAY: What guy?

BOGART: This guy I went to high school.

(BOGART *sits on bed, smiling as he watches* FAY *undress.*)

FAY: Yeah?

BOGART: Hey. You got this milky body. I ever tell you?

FAY: *(Pausing)* Why is it. Whenever I start to undress.
You turn into babyshit.? *(Resuming)* So this guy.

BOGART: *(Glumly)* His father owns a auto repair.

FAY: And? You gonna fix cars?

BOGART: There's no money fixin cars.

FAY: So why bring it up? Jesus. *(In bra and panties by
now, she crosses to bureau, removes article of clothing,
enters bathroom, slamming door.)*

BOGART: Will you lissen to me? Holy shit.

*(Places bottle on nightstand. Removes boots. Rises, stands
before vanity mirror. Looks at himself. Drops vest onto floor,
rubbing his naked torso. Sings, a la Jim Morrison's "Back
Door Man":)* "The men don't know but the little girls/
Unnerstand!" *(He unbuckles belt, loosens pants. Calling
into bathroom:)* Hey. Miss Bonino. You're missin the
show. *(Sinuously he wriggles out of trousers, which drop to
the floor. He is wearing jockies)* Hey. Ta-Da!

*(Enter FAY from bathroom, in scant nightie that leaves her
almost naked, ignoring BOGART. She sits at vanity.)*

*(BOGART, reacting to her indifference, kicks away pants,
goes to bed, sweeps Snoopy pillow onto floor, sits, drinks.)*

BOGART: You young ladies you think…

(FAY is angrily removing make-up.)

BOGART: All night you been snappin at this puttin
me down sayin this is cheap take me into Manhattan.
Every move I make it's like a joke to you. Maybe cause
your dad is back, who knows? But you never care what
a guy has gotta do to show you a good time. All you
do is snap.

FAY: So go home.

BOGART: This *was* my home til your dad come back!

FAY: Don't sit around here suckin on a bottle. You go get a job, Bogart. Even if it's pushin clothes racks? For some Hassid (*Pronounced with no inflection, Queens style, to rhyme with "flaccid"*) on Seventh Avenue.

BOGART: So now I'm this P R workin some Hassid. There must be a kid in your high school's gonna be a dentist you should go for it, Fay. Out here in Queens you got this attitude I don't believe. Your dad's this swabbie and I'm suppose to be in real estate.

FAY: (*Angrily brushing hair*) Shut up on my dad!

BOGART: I said! I know this kid.

FAY: Who?

BOGART: This kid. You lissenin? His old man's auto repair is cavin in. They need somebody.

FAY: Somebody for what?

BOGART: That's my surprise.(*Leaning forward; excitedly*) To drive around at night. You mark a coupla cars. The kids's good. Fast. He could teach me.

(*Beat.* FAY *ceases brushing hair.*)

FAY: (*Into mirror; contemptuously*) Trainee program?

BOGART: A little hotwire you take it back to the shop. Repaint it, maybe rebuild it. It's chocolate cake.

FAY: We could buy a house in Kew Gardens. A little yard. A barbeque. I could take care of the kids. (*Slams down brush*) While you're in jail!

BOGART: It's opportunity! Such a fuckin mouth. Maybe I should work that Hassid, Fay.

FAY: I would rather have you runnin clothes racks, Bogart, than visiting hours at Rikers.

BOGART: Runners can't take you some disco in Manhattan, Fay. You young ladies.

FAY: Don't put it on me.

BOGART: Put what?

FAY: You wanner be a cheap shot? With the stolen cars?
Be a cheap shot. But don't! Blame! *(Mimics)* "The young
ladies!"

BOGART: This United States, Fay. One half of this
United States is bend over for the other half. You
young ladies. You don't know. Know shit. You wait til
you're outa high school. You'll see. Prob'ly end up a
secretary some shit.

FAY: I'm takin shorthand, so what?

BOGART: *(Rises; into her face)* Sit in this office waitin for
Mr Executive to marry you. But I got the New York
Daily News here. You lissenin, Fay?

FAY: I got a choice?

BOGART: You sound Queens you look Queens and no
man! *(Finger in her face)* Is takin you upstairs.

(In central room, ROY *abruptly jerks upright and begins to
sing:)*

ROY: He flies through the air
Wit' the greatest of ease,
The greasy young spic
Onna flyin trapeeze!"

(In bedroom, FAY *and* BOGART *freeze.)*

BOGART: *(Whispering)* I thought you said he was out.

FAY: *(Rising, going to bedroom doorway)* I don't know.

*(*FAY, *with* BOGART *observing over her shoulder, peers into
central room through beaded curtain. Fair lights intensify.*
ROY *is sprawled over table, his fingers wavering at the base
of the bottle. He lurches upright in chair.)*

ROY: Let's see you do it, Jesus. You got halls, you're
this P R with bull balls, I gotta say it. They piss on
you and you turn right around. And piss on them.

It's beautiful. Beautiful. *(Laughing, he rises and crosses staggering to window.)*

BOGART: *(To* FAY, *loud whisper)* This is like. *Twilight Zone.*

*(*FAY *elbows* BOGART *in ribs to shush him.)*

*(*ROY *grips window frame, peering out.)*

ROY: Sure I know it shakes! Leavin a fucky ladder like that, why it's criminal indiff' to the seaman's health, And happiness! *(Chortles uncontrollably)* No. Hey. You go first. *(Sings)* "The greasy young spic—" *(He stiffens, leaning out over fire escape)* Hey! Shipmate! Where the fuck did you go? *(Hissing it:)* Jesus? You down there? What was that noise? Sounded like a bunch of fuckin. Plantains! *(Turns from window, clasping hands to ears)* I hate that noise, sailor! *(Sinks to his knees on floor)* We gotta rest. Gotta sleep on it. Yeah, let's just. You and me. Lay down here. Together. Like shipmates. And wake up in like. In like Tripoli, O K? *(Crumples into fetal position)*

(Beat, as fair lights dim)

FAY: He's out for good now. Til Christmas.

BOGART: I gotta put it to you, Fay. Your old man's a scar-legged drunk of a fuckin guy like I never—

FAY: *(Turning on him) Yeah?* Well, for years that man been goin to sea eatin shit and dreamin his stupid dreams. But Bogart? *(Crosses back to vanity, sits)* He always got on that ship. And did his duty.

BOGART: Oh. Is this like a—personal attack?

FAY: *(Angrily lighting a cigarette)* You're a loser, Bogart.

*(*BOGART *moves to bed, sits at its foot, his back to* FAY *and swigs from bottle.)*

BOGART: Don't put down on me no more, Fay. Cause I need you tonight, Fay. *Bad.*

(FAY *looks at* BOGART *and smokes, the air going out of her rage. Stubs out cigarette*)

FAY: Yeah well. This one's not waitin for some man, Bogart. To take her up or down or anyplace. (*She rises and sits on haunches middle of bed. Smiles, wriggling her behind*) Except maybe to that new disco on Columbus Avenue.

BOGART: (*Over his shoulder*) You fuck.

(FAY *laughs outright, and begins carressing* BOGART'*s back.*)

FAY: I dunno. I hold you you're like a stone. So smooth and hard like a stone I would pick up at the beach.

BOGART: (*Over his shoulder*) So now I'm this thing washed up at Riis Park. Keep talkin, Fay.

FAY: (*Still carressing his back*) You're so damn hard and clean I dunno what it means. I run around all day goin to classes makin plans. How I'm gonna stand in *my* shoes. On *my* feet. In *my* city. How I'm gonna find a good job and do it right.

BOGART: Modelling classes. Fay Bonino. A star of the models.

FAY: (*Still carressing*) Only. I gotta get up every day. And put my face out there. And not see or hear all this shit. I gotta use every ounce of what's hard in me. Then I get itchy. I take you in my arms. And your body's so hard I feel like water. You just drop like a stone into me and I don't know who I am. For what? Maybe five, ten minutes. (*Smiles; her fingers spread hungrily over his back*) I can just give it up. Let it go, all that tightness. (*Shakes her head*) I dunno.

BOGART: You gonna be real unhappy, Fay.

FAY: Bogart? (*Ironic*) That. That job opportunity? (*Beat*) Pass it up.

(BOGART *turns to look at* FAY.)

BOGART: Don't you ever get scared at least?

(FAY *draws* BOGART *to her on the bed.*)

FAY: All the time.

(FAY *and* BOGART *begin making love.*)

(*Lights down on bedroom*)

(*The fair lights intensify on wreckage in central room.*)

(*A blast of Italian rock 'n roll through the open window, and:*)

(*Blackout*)

(*Curtain*)

END OF PLAY

www.ingramcontent.com/pod-product-compliance
Lightning Source LLC
Chambersburg PA
CBHW052212090426
42741CB00010B/2505